奇 山 秀 水

WONDERFUL HILLS
& BEAUTIFUL WATER

奇 山 秀 水

漓江出版社
Lijiang Publishing House

封面題字: 甘樹立(桂林市副市長)
主　　編: 陳小立
副 主 編: 李永剛　陸水保
責任編輯: 趙　濤　滕　彬
撰　　文: 李永剛
策　　劃: 滕　彬
圖片編輯: 呂華昌　陳作慈
裝幀設計: 秦　杰
英文翻譯: 周昱麟　張　征
日文翻譯: 陸建林
攝　　影: 呂華昌　滕　彬　秦　杰　姜　江
　　　　　秦玉庭　林　琳　李亞石　張小林
　　　　　黃富旺　葉建平　金可林

扉　　　書: 甘樹立(桂林市副市長)
編 集 長: 陳小立
副 編 集 長: 李永剛　陸水保
編集責任者: 趙　濤　滕　彬
解 説 文: 李永剛
裝　　幀: レイアウト
日 本 語 翻譯: 陸建林
攝　　　影: 呂華昌　滕　彬　秦　傑　姜　江
　　　　　　秦玉庭　林　琳　李亞石　張小林
　　　　　　黃富旺　葉建平　金可林

In Scripted on Front Cover: By Gan Shu li
　　　　　　　　　　　　(The Vice Mayor of Guilin)
Editor in chief: Chen Xiao li
Deputy Editor in Chief: Li Yong gang, Lu Shui bao
Managing Editor: Zhao tao, Teng bin
Photo Editor: Lu Hua chang
Designed by: Qin Jie
Captoon by: Li Yong gang
English Translator: Zhou Yu lin, Zhang Zheng
Photographers: Lu Hua chang, Teng bin, Qin Jie
　　　　　　　Jiang jiang, Lin Lin, Qin Yu ting,
　　　　　　　Li Ya shi, Zhang Xiao lin,
　　　　　　　Huang Fu wang,
　　　　　　　Ye jian ping, Jin ke lin

前　　言

　　無論你是否到過桂林,游覽過灕江,觀賞過陽朔秀甲天下的風光,《奇山秀水》中的一幅幅美妙的風光將會把你引入山水王國的人間仙境,爲你導游,令你心馳神往,流連忘返。

　　桂林是一座有兩千多年歷史,風景秀麗的歷史文化名城。山青、水秀、洞奇、石美、桂香是她馳名中外的"五絕"。象鼻山、叠彩山、伏波山、蘆笛岩、七星岩、"三山兩洞"的美景使你驚嘆不已。清澈明麗的灕江,像翠綠色玉帶,彎彎曲曲飄舞在萬點奇峰之間;八十三公里水路,把桂林陽朔絢麗多姿的風光連接在一起。灕江兩岸是山水的精華,是充滿着詩情畫意的大自然藝術長廊。冠岩幽境,黄布倒影,畫山觀馬,興坪佳勝,令你如痴如醉。

　　陽朔風光景色迷人,堪稱秀甲桂林。峰巒層叠,江流如帶,山川景色與田園風光交相輝映。碧蓮玉笋、千年古榕樹、陽朔公園、月亮山,想必是你行踪出没之處。

　　《奇山秀水》畫册,沿桂林、灕江、陽朔一攬佳勝,收集風光美景81幅,收集桂北風俗民情9幅,謹以饗游客。

桂林市区鸟瞰
A bird's—eye View of Guilin City.
桂林市町鳥瞰

3

Preface

It is no matter whether you have been to Guilin and visited Lijiang River or Yangshuo scenery, 《The Wonderful Hills And Waters》 will give you a lot of beautiful scenery photographs as a guide to take you to the paradise on earth. The scenery is so beautiful that you'll enjoy yourself so much as to lose yourself in it.

Guilin is a beautiful scenic city with ancient Chinese culture and history of more than 2000 years. The city is well-known both at home and abroad for its five wonderful characteristics: green hills, clear waters, fantastic caves, spectacular rocks and sweet scent of osmanthus. Such as Elephant Trunk Hill, Folded Brocade Hill, Underground Water Hill, Reed Flute Cave and Seven Star Cave, they are known as "Three Hills and Two Caves". The beautiful scenery will make you pleasantly surprise. The clear Lijiang River is like a green jade ribbon floating among thousands of green hills. From Guilin to Yangshuo the Lijiang River traverses 83 kilometres. The either bank of the river affords the most beautiful scendry as a long art gallery with rich natural in poetic and picture. Such as. A Secluded spot of Crown Cave, Reflection of Yellow Beach, Viewing and admiring the stone horses under Paint Cliff, and the beautiful landscape of Xingping Town will make you very glad as if were crazy and drunk.

Yangshuo Landscape is so wonderful that it wins the fame of the best scenic spot in Guilin Area. The green peaks are rising one higher than another, the rivers are like green gauze ribbons floatin among the hills, the rural scenery and hills and rivers add radiance and beauty to each other. The Green Lotus Peak, the Big Banyan which is more than 1500 years old, the Yangshuo Park, the Moon Hill, those are the most famous scenic spots that you would go to visit.

《The Wonderful Hills And Waters》 photograph album contains the beautiful scenery of Guilin, Lijiang River and Yangshuo. There are — scenery photographs and — folk custom photographs in the album, and it is offered to the tourists.

前　書　き

桂林いらっしゃったお客様は、すでに漓江下りをされ、『天下に甲たる山水』の最も美しい陽朔風景を満契されたことと思います。又まだお越しでない方も私どもは中国屈指の観光地、桂林陽朔の素晴らしさをご存じないではないでしょうか。この『奇山秀水』写真集に収められた数数の美しい写真はそんな皆様を山水王国と呼ばれる自然世界の仙郷へと誘います。写真に再現された美しさはご覧になる皆様の心を奪い、時のたつのを忘れさせることでしょう。

桂林は2千年あまりの歴史を持つ、景色の美しい歴史文化名城でございます。数数の奇峰、清く澄んだ水、奇抜な洞窟、美しい岩、かぐわしい秋の木犀、この五つの美は桂林を代表するものでございます。象鼻山、畳彩山、伏波山の三つの山、蘆笛岩、七星岩の二つの洞窟の美景は人人の心を引きつけます。澄み渡る漓江の水はまるでビロードの帯の様に数数奇峰の間を巡り、桂林と陽朔間の83KMをつないでいます。漓江両岸は奇峰の宝庫で、詩的情緒あふれかつ絵の様に美しく、『大自然の芸術画廊』と言ったところです。中でも代表的な景色には『冠岩幽境』『黄布倒影』『画山観馬』『興坪美景』等と呼ばれるものがございます。

陽朔は、その景色の素晴らしさについては桂林以上と言われています。峰峰は重なりあい、川は玉帯の様に流れ、陽朔の田園風景と見事に融合しています、『碧蓮玉筍』『樹齢千年のガジュマルの木』『月の山』これらは観光客の足を奪います。

『奇山秀水』写真集は桂林、漓江、そして陽朔の美を一冊に収めております。風景写真81枚、桂北地区民俗風景写真9枚を集めたこの写真集はきっと皆様に喜んでいただけることと存じます。

微波轻漾黄布滩

Ripples waving on Yellow Cloth Shoal.

静かな波飾られる黄布灘

象鼻山
Elephant Trunk Hill

象鼻山

叠彩晨曦

The morning sunlight over Diecai Hill.

叠彩山朝やけ

7

烟雾轻笼小东江
The Xiaodong River in mist.

霧立ち込める小東江

伏波晚照
Sunset glowing on Fubo Hill.
夜の伏波山

9

南溪山
Nanxi Hill.
南溪山

塔山冬雪
The winter snow covering Pagoda Hill.

冬雪飾られる塔山

流彩飞霞
Rays of sunlight shine through the multicolore
霞が満天

伏波晚照
Sunset glowing on Fubo Hill.
夜の伏波山

南溪山
Nanxi Hill.

南溪山

駱駝山
Camel Hill
駱駝山

奇峰之秋
Autumn in Qifeng Town.

奇峰町の秋

桂林花桥
Guilin Flower Bridge.

桂林花橋

伏波山·试剑石
The Sword Testing Column in Fubo Hill.

伏波山、試劍石

龙隐岩
Longyin Cave (The cave for the dormant dragon).
龍隱岩

南天一柱·独秀峰

The Duxiu Peak is like a Pillar in south sky.

南天一柱、獨秀峰

木龙古塔

Ancient pagoda on Mulong(Wooden Dragon)ferry.

木龍古塔

杉湖·蘑菇亭
The Mushroom Pavilion in Fir Lake.
杉湖、ユッシユルームのような東屋

蘆笛岩
The Reed Flute Cave

蘆笛岩

霞染桃花江
The glory of the dawn is mirrored on Peach Blossom River.
霞のたなびく桃花江

桂林之春
Guilin City in spring.

桂林之夏
Guilin City in summer.

桂林之秋
Guilin City in autumn.

桂林の四季、春、夏、秋冬

桂林之冬
Guilin City in winter.

漓江源头·苗儿山
Miaoer Hill—the fountainhead of Lijiang River. 灕江の源 苗兒山

田家河风光
A wonderful sight of Tianjia River.
田家河の風景

暮
Dusk
夕暮れ

杨堤春色
Spring in Yangdi.
春訪れる楊提

桃红白沙

The red peach blossoms in Baisha Town.

桃の花飾る白沙

浪石风光
The scenery of Langshi.

浪石の風景

九马画山
Painted Cliff with Nine Horses.

九馬畫山

山鎮飛虹

Rainbow over the moutain town　山に訪れる虹

落霞晚舟醉江天
The sunset clouds red over the sky and the boat in the river.
霞赤く染まる空に晩の舟

蓝色印象·下龙

The blue impression of Xialong.

青く澄み渡る下潼景色

漓江晨雾觅仙踪

Seeking the trace of the celestial being in the mist of Lijiang River.

朝霧の灘江に仙郷を偲ぶ

青峰列队，岚影绰绰
The blue hills are standing in a line.
with the refletion in the river
青峰配列、かすみが縹緲

人间仙境今又见，碧莲峰里住人家
Like a paradise on earth in Yangshuo, the households are below the Green Lotus Peak.
人間の仙郷、碧蓮峰に住家

大圩瀑布
The waterfall of Daxiu Town.　大墟の滝

漓江夜泊
Anchoring alongside the shore of Lijiang River in evening.

灘江の夜、停泊する舟

水碧碧山青青
Clear and greenish waters and blue hills.

水清く山青く灘江

春流漓江梦

The Lijiang River flows into your dream, in spring.

春、灘江夢を作り

霞飞高田
Rosy clouds over Gaotian Town.

高田にて美しい霞

群峰竞秀
The green hills rise sharply and compete each other for beauty.
群峰美しさを争って

岁月悠悠

The long time flows away. 　長い長い歳月

44

烟雨漓江
The Lijian River in misty rain.
烟雨灘江

绿野青峰

Green Champaign and blue hills.

绿野に青い峰

冬霧
Winter mist

冬の霧

山涛涌红日

A red sun rises in countless hills.

山々をふちどる朝日

幻影奇波
The fantastic image of wonderful waves.
神秘な波

云水苍茫小楫轻

Light boats in a vast expanse of water and clouds

灕江の雨景色に小舟

一缕金光翠屏幕开

When a wisp of sunlight comes from the blue hills at dawn, a painted screen is open.

一筋光ですばらしい山水を

漓江晨韵
The morning Lingering charm of Lijiang River.

詩情にあふれる灕江の朝

青山挂彩虹

A rainbow hanging on the blue hills.

青山に虹

光坪風光
Xinping Landscape
興坪の風光

漓江鱼鹰
The Cormorants of Lijiang River.

灕江の風景『鵜飼』

漓江田园图
The rural scenery of Lijiang River.

灕江の田園風景、

梦萦奇峰

May be the beautiful hills will go to your dream.

忘れられない奇峰

兴坪僧尼山

Seng-ni (Buddhist monk and nun) Hill of Xingping Town.　興坪の僧と尼山

彩笔绘青山
Beautiful green hills as if been drawn out by colour writing brush.
繪畫的風情の青山

59

烟霞繞奇峰

Peaks surrounded by clouds

もやに立ちこめる奇峰

山重水复

Countless Mountains by the green water surrounded.

重なる山と巡る水

61

漓江放牧图
A picture of herding on the beach of Lijiang River.　瀉江での放牧

碧水滩头阳朔秀
Beautiful Yangshuo Town by the beach of clear Lijiag River.　浅瀬に清い水、陽朔の美景

静静的山川
Still mountains and rivers.

静かな山と川

63

江峰晨曦
Morning sunlight over the blue river and hills.

朝やけに川と峰

萬家燈火
Amyriad of lights
家々に輝く燈光

夏日漓江
Summer in Lijiang River.

夏の灘江

漓江晨雾
The Lijiang River in morning mist.

灕江の朝霧

杜鹃红高田
The red azaleas over the Gaotian town.

高田を彩るつづじの花

漓江月夜
Lijiag River in moon light.
灘江の月夜

余輝

Afterglow

夕暮れ雲間からもれる光線

书童山红叶
Red leaves of Shutong Hill.

書童山にもみじ

船在青山顶上行

The boats flow on the river with the reflection in it just like traveling over the blue hills.

舟が青山の上に浮かぶか

清山晨霁
The clear river flows after rain in morning.

きれい川の曙

73

漓江春雨谣

A rhyme of Lijiang River in spring rain

灘江の春雨

一弯青山绿水
A bend in the greenish river with blue hills.

曲がりくねる川に峰峰

阳朔卓笔峰

Zhuobi Peak in Yangshuo (A peak shaped like an inverted Chinese writing brush).

陽朔の卓筆峰

青崖渡之晨
Morning of Qinge Ferry.
青崖渡し場の朝

悄逝的清流
The clear river flowed quietly and sluggishly.

静かに流れる清流

山光水影浅草滩
The reflections of blue hills in the water by the grass beach.

山青水秀の淺瀬

竹影山光伴碧水

The shadow of bamboo and green hills by the clear waters.

竹林、青山、澄み渡る山水

程阳风雨桥
Wind and Rain Bridge of Chengyang.

風雨橋、(程陽町にて)

龙脊梯田
Terraced fields of Longji.

段々畑、

侗寨人家
Households of Dong Nationality stockaded village.

侗族の村落、

壮寨小景
Scenery of Zhuang stockaded village.

壮族の村景色

82

苗妹梳妆
Miao Nationality girls are dressing and making up.
身支度する苗族の娘

多耶舞
The dance of Duoye.
侗族歌踊"多耶舞"

小小芦笙手
Young players of Lusheng (A reedpipe wind instrument).
蘆笙奏でる少年

侗族拦路歌
The Dong Nationality girls singing the song for blocking the way.
歓迎の歌を歌う人々

织侗锦

Weaving brocade of Dong Nationality.

錦織り(侗族)

（桂）新登字 03 号

奇 山 秀 水

*

漓江出版社出版

（广西桂林市南环路 159—1 号）

邮政编码：541002

桂林市新华书店发行　　广东粤中印刷公司印刷

*

开本 787×1092　1/24　印张　　　插页 86 字数

1994 年 4 月第 1 版　　1994 年 4 月第 1 次印刷

印数：1—6,000 册

ISBN7—5407—1576—6/J・96

003500

Dear American people:

This is Wei te Zhang (Foster). I'm an exchang student from China. This book is about the supreme scenic beauty of Gui Lin (city), where I use to Live. I really want American people to understand my homeland more and more, because I love it there so much! I just want to say welcome to China, welcome to GuiLin, there are not only scenic beauty, but also very nice Chines people are waiting for you, your family, your friends to visit! You'll have a great time! Absolutely will!

Sincerely: ————— Foster

張 維 特

Zhang, Wei te

written in Cottage Grove, Oregon.

10/22/98